BRANCH LINES AROUND MIDHURST

Vic Mitchell and Keith Smith

A sequel to Branch Lines to Midhurst

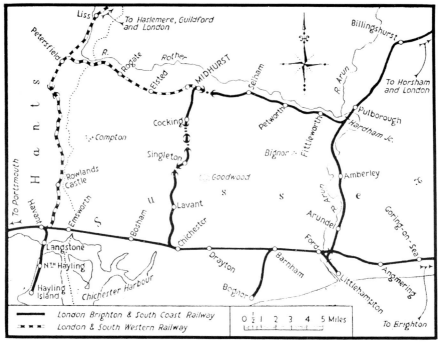

(Railway Magazine)

Design – Deborah Goodridge

First published September 1987

ISBN 0 906520 49 5

© Middleton Press, 1987

Typeset by CitySet - Bosham 573270

Published by Middleton Press
        Easebourne Lane
        Midhurst, West Sussex
        GU29 9AZ
        ☎ 073 081 3169

Printed & bound by Biddles Ltd,
        Guildford and Kings Lynn

CONTENTS

INDEX

ACKNOWLEDGEMENTS

We would like to thank those whose names appear in the photograph credits for help so freely given and also Lord Egremont (for use of the handbills), H.N. James, P. Jerrome, J.R.W. Kirkby, A. Lambert, R. Randell, E. Staff, N. Stanyon, and the West Sussex Record Office (for use of the Garland collection).

Photographs taken by the late E. Wallis are reproduced by permission of Mrs. M. Mason and Mr. D. Wallis; the tickets have been provided by G. Croughton and N. Langridge, while our wives have again been most helpful.

INTRODUCTION

In 1981, we compiled *Branch Lines to Midhurst* and decided to have it published to coincide with the events we were arranging to mark the centenary of the Chichester to Midhurst line. It being rejected by several publishers, Vic Mitchell decided to publish it under the imprint of his Middleton Press.

The initial demand was spectacular and it continues to sell well, month in and month out, over 8000 copies having now been purchased. This album contains a selection from the hundreds of photographs we could not include. Most of them have not been in print before but a few old ones are included in larger and clearer form.

We were reluctant to include maps of every station in our first album but subsequent reaction has shown that this aid to photograph interpretation is appreciated. We therefore offer one, or more, at each location in this volume.

We continue to use a heavy weight paper to avoid print showing through and a non-gloss finish to eliminate reflected light, which prevents full enjoyment of the pictures.

We would like to thank again all those who have expressed their appreciation of the series and who have contributed photographs.

GEOGRAPHICAL SETTING

The Petersfield to Pulborough line ran almost the full length of the Rother Valley, roughly parallel to the escarpment of the South Downs. For most of its length it ran close to or on the sandy deposits of the Folkestone Beds, which provided some revenue from sand traffic, particularly to Croydon. In the Rogate-Elsted area the line traversed Gault Clay, which was used for making red bricks, another source of railway income. North of Hardham Junction, the route crossed the flood plain and alluvial deposits of the River Arun, near its confluence with the Rother.

The Midhurst to Chichester line crossed the geological strata at right angles. It soon left the Folkestone Beds to cross about a mile of Gault Clay. It was here that five brickworks were established to produce the millions of bricks required to line the tunnels and build the bridges of this heavily engineered route. Cocking, like the other Down-foot villages, is situated on a shelf of Upper Greensand. From here the railway pierced the chalk of the South Downs by means of three tunnels before reaching the flint-rich gravels around Lavant. These deposits are still an important part of the economic geology of the area and local railway revenue.

All maps in this album are to the scale of 25" to one mile, unless otherwise stated.

HISTORICAL BACKGROUND

The London & South Western Railway was the first company to run trains to Midhurst, commencing on 1st September 1864, its "Portsmouth Direct" line having opened between Godalming and Havant in 1859.

The London Brighton and South Coast Railway extended its Horsham branch to Petworth on 10th October 1859 and eventually to its own terminus at Midhurst on 15th October 1866. The two termini were connected by a line on a bridge over Bepton Road capable of carrying the weight of only a single wagon, so that through trains were not possible.

In 1864, the Chichester and Midhurst Railway was authorised and work started in 1865. By 1868 funds were exhausted and partly completed earthworks were abandoned. The scheme was revived in 1876 and the LBSCR arranged to operate the line, which came into use on 11th July 1881.

Midhurst thus became the frontier town between the territories of the two rival companies until they were incorporated into the Southern Railway on 1st January 1923. It was not until 12th July 1925 that the SR replaced the Bepton Road bridge and closed the former LSWR station.

Little changed until passenger services were withdrawn between Midhurst and Chichester on 6th July 1935. Freight services ceased at Cocking and Singleton on 28th August 1953.

Passenger operation between Petersfield and Pulborough and goods services between Petersfield and Midhurst ceased on 5th February 1955. The goods yard at Selham and Fittleworth closed in May 1963; at Midhurst on 16th October 1964 and at Petworth on 20th May 1966.

Lavant remained in use for freight until 3rd August 1968 and for sugar beet until January 1970. In 1972, the line was reopened as far as Snakes Lane bridge (now Hunters Race) for use by a block train of hopper wagons carrying unprocessed gravel to Drayton, east of Chichester.

In 1986, an investigation was made into the possibility of reopening the Lavant to Singleton section and there appears to be almost total approval for the scheme. A number of trial borings for oil in the district have proved encouraging and so there is a possibility that part of one of the branch lines to Midhurst might be required again.

PASSENGER SERVICES

LSWR (1864 - 1922)

Weekday services, in the first decade, consisted of five return journeys, this gradually increasing to eleven by 1913. World War I caused a reduction to six in 1917 but, by 1922, the service level had returned to ten.

In many of the early years, no Sunday trains were operated but later three trains each way were provided and in some Edwardian years there were four. From 1919 onwards two of the services operated to and from Portsmouth & Southsea.

LBSCR (1859 - 1922)

The initial weekday timetable showed five trains to and from Petworth. The frequency was increased to eight upon extension to Midhurst, but two trains terminated at Petworth and two trips were run on Sundays. This level of service was maintained on the Pulborough - Midhurst line throughout the period, apart from curtailments during World War I. An interesting feature of the 1864 timetable was the dropping of a slip coach from the 4.05 London Bridge to Portsmouth express at 5.28, allowing Midhurst residents to arrive undisturbed at 5.55. Another notable train was the 7.00 am (Mondays only) departure from Midhurst in 1910 which ran to Three Bridges, where "weekenders" could make a good connection for London.

The Chichester - Midhurst route had a weekday service of six trains, which was reduced to five after World War I. Three journeys on Sundays were operated for a few years prior to that war when there was also an extra train on Wednesdays, for Chichester market. Most trains ran to and from Pulborough with the 8.15 am from Chichester running through to Victoria until March 1929.

SR (1923-47)

The frequency on the Petersfield line was increased to 12, with three on Sundays unchanged. In the early 1930's, the service was gradually reduced and this eliminated the need to cross passenger trains at Rogate. The Sunday trains were increased to five by 1937.

The Chichester line timetable remained little changed, until services ceased in 1935.

The Pulborough route had eight or nine trains on weekdays, of which one ran to Dorking North, until July 1938. Sunday services increased from three to five, during the 1940s.

Reorganisation of the timetables took place in 1926, when rail motor (push-pull) working commenced and in 1937-38, when electrification of the main lines necessitated revised connectional times. This resulted in many trains waiting for long periods at Midhurst, much to the annoyance of the small number of through passengers, and some trains terminated there.

BR (1948-55)

No alteration was made to the basic frequency of nine trains each way, although the 7.56 am from Pulborough was eventually withdrawn. Sunday trains ceased in 1951.

1890

THE TUNNELS

	Length yards	Gradient northwards	Use after closure
West Dean	445	1 in 75 up	Building storage
Singleton*	741	1 in 100 up	Mushroom farming
Cocking*	738	1 in 60 down	–

*Fitted with steel doors during WWII to protect naval ammunition trains stored therein. The doors remain in situ.

MIDHURST and PETERSFIELD—Southern.

Miles	Up.	Week Days. mrn	mrn	mrn	mrn	mrn		aft	aft	aft	aft	aft	aft	aft		Sundays. mrn		aft	c
—	Midhurst ....dep.	6 53	7 59	8 54	9 32	11 5	....	12 9	2 1	3 18	4 40	5 56	7 5	8 15	....	7 30	....	3 20	6 15
3	Elsted	6 59	8 5	9 0	9 38	1111	....	1215	2 7	3 24	4 46	6 2	7 11	8 21	....	7 36	....	3 26	6 21
5	Rogate, for Harting	7 7	8 12	9 5	9 43	1116	....	1220	2 12	3 29	4 53	6 7	7 16	8 23	....	7 44	....	3 31	6 29
9½	Petersfield 178, *above* .... arr.	7 20	8 24	9 16	9 53	1126	....	1230	2 22	3 33	5 5	6 17	7 26	8 36	....	7 57	....	3 41	6 42
28	178 Portsmouth & Southsea arr.	8 43	9 19	1028	1035	1221	*a*	1J19	3F4	4H41	5 48	7*d*2	8K12	9N39	....	9 1	....	4 53	7 38
64½	London (Waterloo) .... "	9 12	9 52	1116	....	1 6	....	4J0	5 2	5 41	7 6	9 26	....	1020	....	1016	....	6 15	8 52

a Arrives at 12 19 aft. on Saturdays.
c Thro' Train to Portsmouth and Southsea.
d Arrives at 7 11 aft. on Saturdays.
F Arrives at 3 17 aft. on Saturdays.
H Arrives at 4 25 aft. on Saturdays.
J Arrives Portsmouth and Southsea at 1 50 and London (W.) at 4 13 aft. on Saturdays by changing at Surbiton.
K Arrives at 8 21 aft. on Saturdays.
N Arrives at 9 21 aft. on Saturdays.

1924

PULBOROUGH, MIDHURST, and CHICHESTER.—Southern

Miles from Pulboro'.	Down.	Week Days. mrn	mrn	mrn	mrn		aft	aft	aft	aft		Sundays. mrn	mrn		aft	
	210 Victoria ....dep.	6 20	9 0	1010	1120	....	1 20	4 20	4 53	7 20	....	6 55	8 18	....	7 0	....
	210 London Bridge .... "	6 35	8 40	1020	1110	....	....	....	5 5	7 15	....	7 2	8 25	....	6 38	....
	Pulborough ....dep.	8 20	11 0	1215	2 3	....	3 12	5 55	7 5	9 15	....	9 30	4 17	....	9 4	....
2½	Fittleworth	8 28	11 6	1222	2 10	....	3 21	6 2	7 13	9 22	....	9 37	4 25	....	9 15	....
5¼	Petworth	8 35	1112	1228	2 16	....	3 29	6 9	7 20	9 28	....	9 43	4 31	....	9 23	....
7½	Selham	8 41	1118	1234	2 22	....	3 37	6 16	7 27	9 35	....	9 50	4 37	....	9 30	....
11	Midhurst † 178 .... arr.	8 49	1125	1242	2 30	....	3 45	6 24	7 35	9 43	....	9 58	4 45	....	9 40	....
	Midhurst † 178 .... dep.	8 56	1127	1256	....	....	4 22	6 25	....	....	....	....	....	....	....	....
13½	Cocking	9 3	1134	1 3	....	....	4 28	6 32	....	....	....	....	....	....	....	....
16¼	Singleton	9 11	1141	1 10	....	....	4 35	6 39	....	....	....	....	....	....	....	....
19½	Lavant	9 18	1147	1 17	....	....	4 43	6 45	....	....	....	....	....	....	....	....
23	Chichester 210, 213, arr	9 25	1155	1 25	....	....	4 51	6 53	....	....	....	....	....	....	....	....

Miles	Up.	Week Days. mrn	Thro' Train, Midhurst to Victoria, see page 213.	mrn	mrn	mrn	aft	aft	aft	aft	aft	Sundays. mrn	mrn		aft	
	Chichester ....dep.	....		8 15	9 35	1045	1218	1 58	....	5 45	7 25	....	....	....	....	....
3¼	Lavant	....		8 23	9 41	1052	1224	2 6	....	5 53	7 32	....	....	....	....	....
6¼	Singleton	....		8 32	9 49	11 0	1232	2 14	....	6 1	7 40	....	....	....	....	....
9½	Cocking	....		8 40	9 56	11 7	1239	2 22	....	6 9	7 47	....	....	....	....	....
12	Midhurst † 178 .... arr.	....		8 47	10 2	1113	1245	2 28	....	6 15	7 53	....	....	....	....	....
	Midhurst † 178 .... dep.	7 25		9 17	10 3	1130	1255	2 32	4 28	6 27	7 55	6 50	1010	....	4 55	....
15½	Selham	7 34		9 25	1011	1136	1 2	2 40	4 38	6 35	8 2	7 0	1017	....	5 5	....
17½	Petworth	7 41		9 32	1017	1142	1 8	2 47	4 47	6 41	8 8	7 8	1023	....	5 13	....
20½	Fittleworth	7 49		9 41	1023	1148	1 14	2 54	4 55	6 47	8 14	7 16	1029	....	5 21	....
23	Pulborough 210, 213 arr.	7 57		9 49	1031	1155	1 22	3 2	5 4	6 55	8 22	7 24	1037	....	5 29	....
73	213 London Bridge .... arr.	10 0		12 2	1215	3 32	4 3	....	....	....	10 8	1011	....	....	7 56	....
73¾	213 Victoria .... "	1028		1142	1210	3 32	....	4 45	6 56	....	10 1	1013	....	....	7 32	....

1924

1938

LONDON, PULBOROUGH, MIDHURST, PETERSFIELD, and LONDON.

Miles	Down.	Week Days. mrn	mrn	mrn		mrn	mrn	mrn	mrn		aft	aft	aft	aft		aft	aft	aft	aft	aft	aft				
	Victoria 158 ....dep.	..	..	..	..	..	..	9 18	1118	..	12H18	..	2 18	..	..	4 18	..	6 18	..	8 18	Weds. and Sats.	..	..	..	..
	London Bridge 158 "	..	..	6 16	..	..	..	9*15	11†2	..	12 18	..	2†2	..	..	4†L7	..	6*SO11	..	8†2		..	..	..	..
	Pulborough 159 .... arr.	..	..	7 53	..		..	1030	1230	..	1 53	..	3 30	..	..	5 30	..	7 30	..	9 30		..	..	..	..
—	Pulborough ....dep.	..	..	7 56	..	8 15	..	1035	1235	..	1 56	..	3 35	..	..	5 35	..	7 35	..	9 35		..	..	..	..
2¼	Fittleworth	..	..	8 2	..	8 22	..	1041	1241	..	2 2	..	3 42	..	..	5 41	..	7 41	..	9 41		..	..	..	..
5¼	Petworth	..	..	8 8	..	8 28	..	1047	1247	..	2 9	..	3 47	..	..	5 47	..	7 47	..	9 47		..	..	..	..
7¼	Selham	..	..	8 14	..	8 36	..	1053	1253	..	2 15	..	3 53	..	..	5 53	..	7 53	..	9 53		..	..	..	..
11	Midhurst .... arr.	..	..	8 22	..	8 44	..	11 0	1 0	..	2 24	..	4 1	..	..	6 0	..	8 0	..	10 0		..	..	..	..
	Midhurst .... dep.	7 8	8 11	..	..	..	9 33	11 1	1 1	..	..	3 46	..	5 2	..	..	7 10	..	8 10	..	10 3	..	..	..	..
14¼	Elsted	7 17	8 20	..	..	..	9 42	1111	1 11	..	..	3 55	..	5 11	..	..	7 19	..	8 19	..	1012	..	..	..	..
16¼	Rogate, for Harting	7 21	8 24	.	..	..	9 46	1115	1 15	..	..	3 59	..	5 15	..	..	7 23	..	8 23	..	1016	..	..	..	..
20¼	Petersfield 361, 364 arr.	7 32	8 35	..	..	..	9 57	1126	1 26	..	..	4 10	..	5 26	..	..	7 34	..	8 34	..	1027	..	..	..	..
—	Petersfield 364 ....dep.	7 54	8 45	..	..	..	10 0	1130	1 30	..	..	4 30	..	5 30	..	..	8 0	..	9 0	..	1030	..	..	..	..
73½	Waterloo 364 .... arr.	9 10	9 49	..	..	..	11C46	1254	2 54	..	..	5 54	..	6 54	..	..	9 46	..	1046	..	12 0	..	..	..	..

Miles	Up.	Week Days. mrn	mrn	mrn	mrn	mrn	mrn	mrn	mrn	mrn		aft	aft	aft	aft	aft	aft	aft	aft	aft	aft	aft	aft		
	Waterloo 361 ....dep.	..	..	5 27	..	6 57	..	8 50	..	1050	..	..	..	1250	1 20	2 50	..	4 50	5 20	6*n*20	..	7 50	..	..	..
	Petersfield 361 .... arr.	..	.	7 14	..	8 44	..	1014	..	1214	..	..	..	2 14	2 35	4 14	..	6 14	6 36	7*n*35	..	9 14	..	..	..
—	Petersfield ....dep	6 33	..	7 37	..	8 50	..	1020	..	1219	..	..	..	2 35	2 40	4 18	..	6 35	6 39	7 39	..	9 20	..	..	..
4¼	Rogate, for Harting	6 43	..	7 47	..	9 0	..	1030	..	1229	..	..	..	2 45	2 50	4 28	..	6 45	6 49	7 49	..	9 30	..	..	..
6¼	Elsted	6 47	..	7 51	..	9 7	..	1034	..	1233	..	..	..	2 49	2 54	4 32	..	6 49	6 53	7 53	..	9 34	..	..	..
9¼	Midhurst .... arr.	6 57	..	8 1	..	9 20	..	1044	..	1243	..	..	.	2 59	3 4	4 42	..	6 59	7 8	8 3	..	9 44	..	..	..
	Midhurst .... dep.	..	7 28	..	8 52	..	9 43	..	1145	..	..	1 11	2 45	Except Saturdays.	Saturdays only.	4 45	6 45	Saturdays only.	Except Saturdays.	..	8 45	Weds. and Sats.	10 15	..	..
13	Selham	..	7 36	..	8 59	..	9 50	..	1152	..	..	1 18	2 52			4 52	6 52			..	8 52		10SO22	..	..
15¼	Petworth	..	7 43	..	9 6	..	9 57	..	1159	..	..	1 25	2 59			4 59	6 59			..	8 59		10 28	..	..
17½	Fittleworth	..	7 51	..	9 13	..	10 6	..	12 6	..	..	1 32	3 6			5 6	7 6			..	9 6		..	..	..
20¼	Pulborough A 159, 196 ar.	..	7 58	..	9 21	..	10 14	..	1214	..	..	1 40	3 14			5 14	7 14			..	9 14		10 44	..	..
—	Pulborough 196 ....dep.	..	8 5	..	9 25	..	10 25	..	1225	..	..	1 48	3 25			5 25	7 25			..	9 25		10 58	..	..
72	London Bridge 197 arr.	..	9 38	..	10*40	..	12†L7	..	1*51	..	..	3 35	4*49			7**d*2	9†7			..	10*51		12 36	..	..
70¼	Victoria 197 .... "	..	9*b*33	..	10 31	..	11 40	..	1 40	..	..	3*42	4 40			6 40	8 40			..	10 40		12*40	..	..

Down.	Sundays. mrn		aft	aft	aft		aft	aft	aft			
Victoria 158 ....dep.	7 46	..	..	3U18	..	..	..	7Y18	..	..	..	..
London Bridge 158 "	7*40	..	..	3 16	..	..	..	7 16	..	..	..	..
Pulborough 159 .... arr.	9 23	..	..	4 53	..	..	..	8 54	..	..	..	..
Pulborough ....dep.	9 35	..	..	5 24	..	..	..	9 23	..	..	..	..
Fittleworth	9 41	..	..	5 30	..	..	..	9 30	..	..	..	..
Petworth	9 47	..	..	5 37	..	..	..	9 36	..	..	..	..
Selham	9 53	..	..	5 43	..	..	..	9 43	..	..	..	..
Midhurst .... arr.	10 0	..	..	5 51	..	..	..	9 52	..	..	..	..
Midhurst .... dep.	10 2	..	12 2	..	6 2	..	7 48	..	10 2	..	..	..
Elsted	1011	..	1211	..	6 11	..	7 57	..	1011	..	..	..
Rogate, for Harting	1015	..	1215	..	6 15	..	8 1	..	1015	..	..	..
Petersfield 361 364 arr.	1026	..	1226	..	6 26	..	8 12	..	1026	..	..	..
Petersfield 364 ....dep.	1030	..	1230	..	6 30	..	8 30	..	1030	..	..	..
Waterloo 364 .... arr.	1154	..	1 54	..	7 54	..	9 54	..	12 0	..	..	..

Up.	Sundays. mrn	mrn		aft	aft	aft		
Waterloo 361 ....dep.	..	9 50	..	2 50	5 50	6 50	..	..
Petersfield 361 .... arr.	..	1114	..	4 14	7 14	8 14	..	..
Petersfield ....dep.	6 17	1120	..	4 20	7 17	8 20	..	..
Rogate, for Harting	6 27	1130	..	4 30	7 27	8 30	..	..
Elsted	6 31	1134	..	4 34	7 31	8 34	..	..
Midhurst .... arr.	6 41	1144	..	4 44	7 41	8 44	..	..
Midhurst .... dep.	6 43	..	..	4 45	..	8 45	..	..
Selham	6 51	..	..	4 52	..	8 52	..	..
Petworth	6 58	..	..	4 59	..	8 59	..	..
Fittleworth	7 6	..	..	5 6	..	9 6	..	..
Pulborough A 159, 196 ar.	7 14	..	..	5 14	..	9 14	..	..
Pulborough 196 ....dep.	7 25	..	..	5 22	..	9 25	..	..
London Bridge 197 arr.	9*10	..	..	7*10	..	11†11	..	..
Victoria 197 .... "	9 5	..	..	7 6	..	10 44	..	..

NOTES.

A Station for Storrington (5 miles).
b Dep. Pulborough 8 23 mrn.
C Arr. 11 25 mrn. on Saturdays.
d 5 mins. later on Saturdays.
H Arr. Pulborough 1 30 aft.
L 5 mins. *earlier* on Saturdays.
n Dep. Waterloo 5 50 and arr. Petersfield 7 14 aft on Saturdays.
SO Saturdays only.
SX Saturdays excepted.
U Arr. Pulborough 4 30 aft.
Y Arr. Pulborough 8 30 aft.

* Change at East Croydon.
† Change at Sutton.

PROPOSED BRANCH LINES AROUND MIDHURST

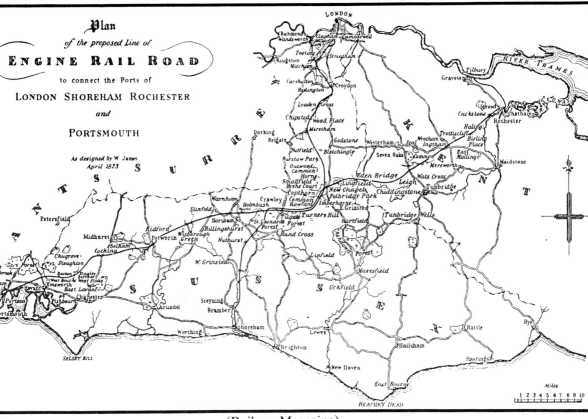

(Railway Magazine)

A large number of railway schemes were put forward for railways passing through the Midhurst district, particularly during the Railway Mania of the mid-1840s and later, during the early 1860s. We have selected three particularly interesting ones, which range over a period of 80 years.

In 1823, at the dawn of the railway age, Mr. W. James drew up a scheme to connect the Metropolis with the ports of Shoreham, Rochester and Portsmouth. The early map of the South Eastern Railway was of similar shape, around 40 years later. A main line ran south from London to Redhill, from where branches diverged to Dover and Reading.

Had Mr. James' plans come to fruition, Petworth might have developed like Haywards Heath and Cocking could have become another Burgess Hill, such has been the effect of main lines on local development.

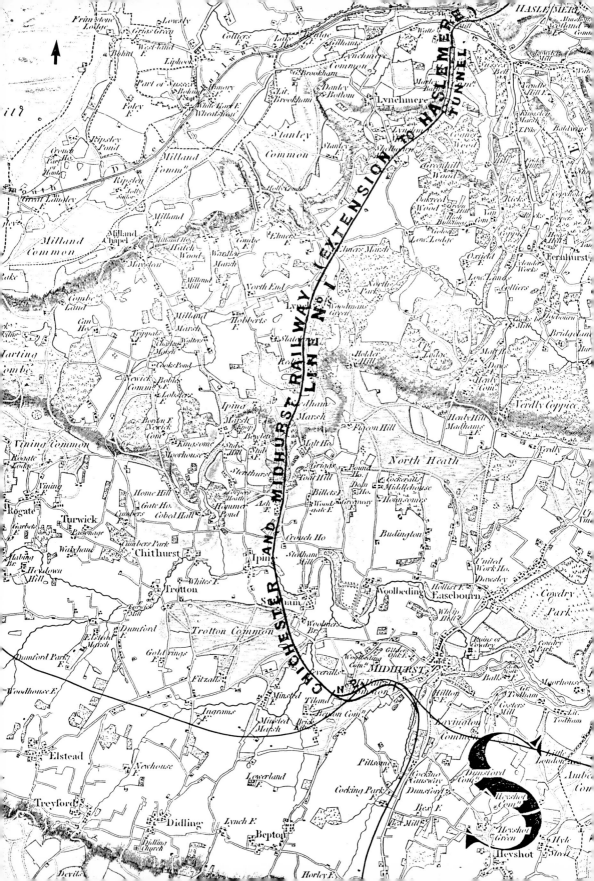

←

While work had commenced on the Chichester & Midhurst Railway, the directors obtained an Act in July 1865 to extend their railway north to Haslemere. The 1″ to 1 mile map shows that, at Midhurst, it would run parallel to the existing railways, with a spur line connecting into the LBSCR terminus. It would then cross over the LSWR line on a bridge and a trailing connection would be provided to that company's station.

After crossing the undulating common land, a new station would be reached at Stedham. Thereafter a climb at 1 in 70 for nearly two miles was proposed. A further station was planned near Redford and a longer climb at 1 in 150 and some length at 1 in 70 would lead to a tunnel 1089 yds long, under Marley Heights.

The last part of the route was close to Marley Lane and Shottermill Ponds, finishing along the route of the present Kings Road.

→

In 1902, the Surrey & Sussex Light Railway was proposed by H.F. Stephens, better known now as the Colonel Stephens, whose rambling, rustic railways are featured in our *Branch Line to Selsey* and *Branch Line to Tenterden* albums. This rural backwater was to commence at a triangular junction west of Selham; run down at 1 in 50, cross the River Rother and climb up at 1 in 50, to a station near Lodsworth.

An undulating path was to be followed to Cranleigh, where a junction would be made with the LBSCR. A further five miles of line was proposed from there to Ockley, with a station south of Ewhurst.

The mileages shown are from Cranleigh and are superimposed on the 1898 survey, at 1″ to 1 mile.

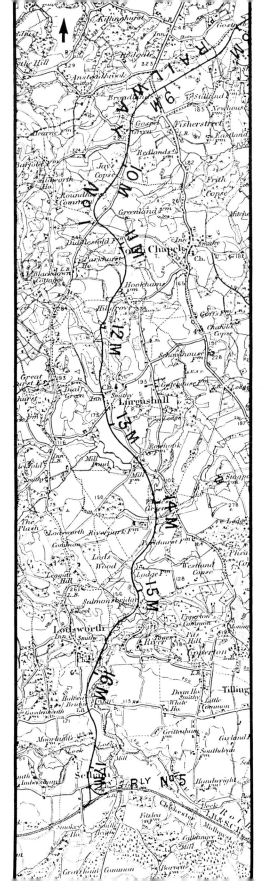

1. Pulborough towards Midhurst

PULBOROUGH

1. Pulborough and Billingshurst were the only intermediate stations when the branch was extended from Horsham to Petworth in 1859. Pulborough station remains largely intact today, along with the integral goods shed which is obscured by trees in this view. (Lens of Sutton)

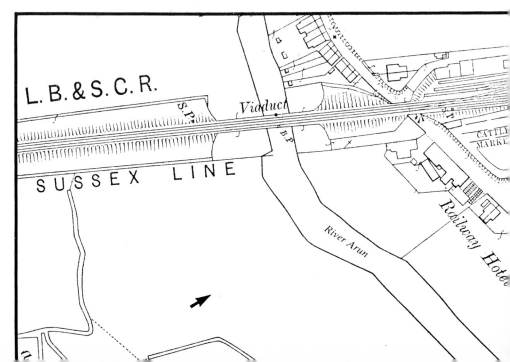

2. The loop line was normally used by the Midhurst branch trains, but the turntable by the water tower was little used in latter years as most services were push-pull operated. (E.R. Lacey/R.C. Riley collection)

1911 edition shows that cattle were segregated from goods and passenger traffic, as at Selham.

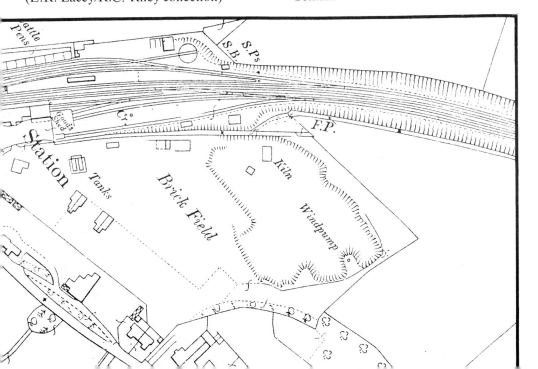

3. A southward view in 1924 shows the nameboard to be beyond the end of the up platform. It could not remain there when the platform was extended prior to electrification in 1938. The subway was also lengthened at that time – the new part being obvious to this day. (F.W. Spry/E.R. Lacey collection)

SUMMARY OF CHIEF TRAFFIC. MIDHURST BRANCH LINES. 1938.

| Station. | Tkt. Issue. | Tkts. Coll. | Seasons. | Parcels | | Horses | | Wagons | | Wagons |
				In.	Out.	In.	Out.	In.	Out.	Live Stock.
...idhurst	5,618	10,660	5	19,058	2,499	360	487	3,401	3,940	73
...lham	1,450	2,226	2	2,386	199	5	12	297	712	12
...tworth	2,709	4,369	38	10,430	1,354	133	233	1,706	209	80
...ttleworth	1,415	2,460	23	1,344	760	2	2	319	145	46
...sted	2,660	3,342	9	842	121	6	5	295	67	16
...gate	3,995	5,054	18	1,738	379	12	10	467	109	3
...cking	—	—	—	—	—	—	—	258	2	4
...vant	—	—	—	603	36	85	87	171	130	74
...ngleton	—	—	—	1,050	76	48	47	200	344	8
Total ...	17,847	28,111	95	37,451	5,424	651	883	7,114	5,658	316
	*		†		42,875		1,534			

* Not including issue at Petersfield by Guards. † Not including H.O. issue.

...o tons perishable traffic in and out on branch. In 15. Out 71. 1,597 tons of timber ex Singleton, and by the end of September,
...474 tons of sugar beet off the branch. 316 wagons. 1939, this figure was exceeded.
864 tons of fencing ex Selham.

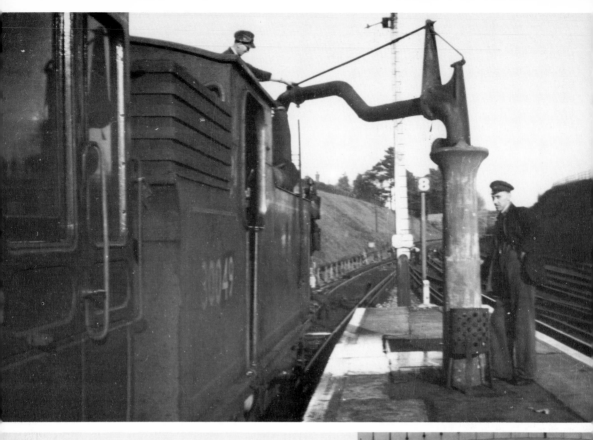

4. As can be seen in this December 1954 photograph, the loop was electrified but the conductor rail was subsequently removed and the line now serves as an engineer's siding, having been truncated at the south end. No. 30049 was one of a number of class M7 0–4–4Ts to work on the branch service. (J. Scrace)

6. Steam is to be found again near Pulborough, at Cheals Garden and Leisure Centre on the road to Petworth. The gauge is 7¼″ and the locomotive is a 4–4–4 of East African style. (V. Mitchell)

5. No. 30049 partly obscures the goods shed but allows us to observe that there are three different styles of canopy over the platforms and yet a fourth beyond the parcel lorry. (J.A.G. Coltas)

HARDHAM JUNCTION

7. The reverse curves evident on the main line resulted from the Arundel route being, historically, a branch from the Petworth line. A London Bridge to Bognor Regis service passes over the level crossing on 28th May 1950. Note the "stilts" under the signal box – one of the last to show this feature. (D. Cullum)

8. Class M7 no. 30027 nears the end of its journey from Midhurst, as it leaves the junction box in the background. For over 120 years the main line was incorrectly described as the *Mid-Sussex*. On 24th March 1986, it was officially and more accurately renamed the Arun Valley Line. (Pamlin Prints).

The 1911 map shows a siding to a brick-works and the single line diverging to Midhurst. Just off the map, it passed through the site of a *Roman Station*, the first staging post on Stane Street, north of Chichester.

Other views and maps of Pulborough and Hardham Junction are to be found in our *Branch Lines to Midhurst*, and *Crawley to Littlehampton* albums.

1922 Appendix to the service timetable.

Pulborough : Hardham Junction, Brick Coy.'s Siding.—This Siding is connected with the Up Midhurst Single Line and is worked from Hardham Junction Signal Box. It holds 14 wagons and the shunting is performed by the Branch Line Goods Trains. The key of the gate is held at the Signal Box and this gate must be secured by the Guard after the work at the Sidings is finished and the key returned to the Signal Box.

Disc Signals are provided to enter and leave the Sidings.

A public footpath crosses this Siding and a lookout must be kept during shunting operations for persons using this footpath. Trucks left in the Sidings must stand clear of this path.

FITTLEWORTH

9. Although the route opened in 1859, a station was not provided until 2nd September 1889. This photograph was taken seven years later, looking east.
(Mrs. G.J. Smith collection)

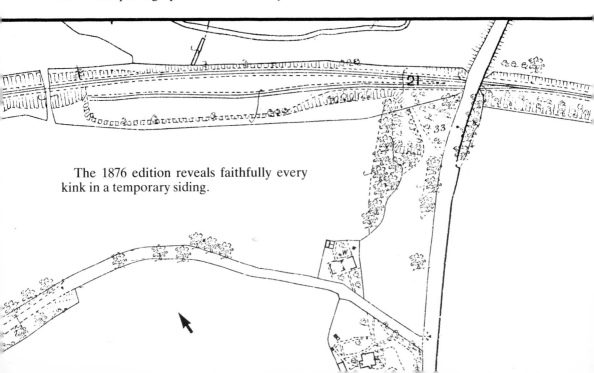

The 1876 edition reveals faithfully every kink in a temporary siding.

10. The signal box was not a block post and was replaced by a ground frame in about 1930. The queue of milk churns is a reminder of this once important source of railway revenue. (Lens of Sutton)

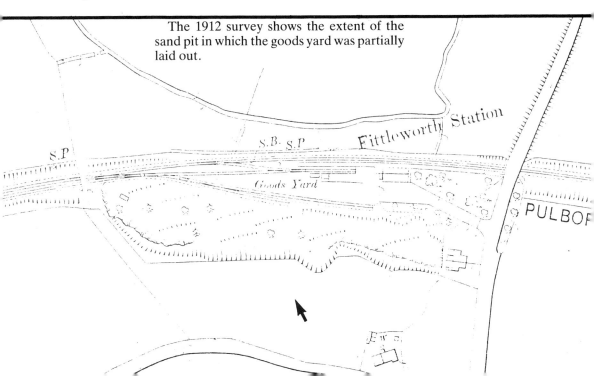

The 1912 survey shows the extent of the sand pit in which the goods yard was partially laid out.

11. Looking west under the B2138 road bridge on 28th May 1950, we see class M7 no. 30027 pausing at the platform and note that the canopy did not reach the platform edge. A similar deficiency is to be found on the up platform at St. Denys. (D. Cullum)

→

12. The nearby River Rother often floods the fields on the right – water was still standing by the tree when this photograph of no. 30047 was taken from the road bridge on 14th April 1952. (D. Cullum)

L. B. & S. C. RY.
Available on the DATE of issue ONLY
This Ticket is issued subject to the Regulations
& Conditions stated in the Company's Time
Tables & Bills.
VICTORIA
TO
SELHAM se
4s.7d. THIRD CL. 4s⁷ᵈ
7143

→

13. The timber-built structure was similar in design to contemporary erections still to be found at Hampden Park and Wivelsfield. The occupation bridge in the background spanned the shunting neck in addition to the line to Petworth. (S.C. Nash)

14. The exterior was similar to that at Selham, as was the small goods shed in the yard. When photographed in 1957 the sign had been removed, the third chimney stack having been demolished about 30 years earlier. (R.A. Holder)

15. The goods yard had been closed three years before freight services to Petworth were withdrawn in May 1966. The demolition men moved in a few weeks later. Twenty years on the planners still fail to recognise the importance of the building in the history of the district, preferring it to fall into further ruin. (J.A.M. Vaughan)

Stop Press – On 2nd July 1987, consent to convert the station into a dwelling was given, following an appeal.

PETWORTH

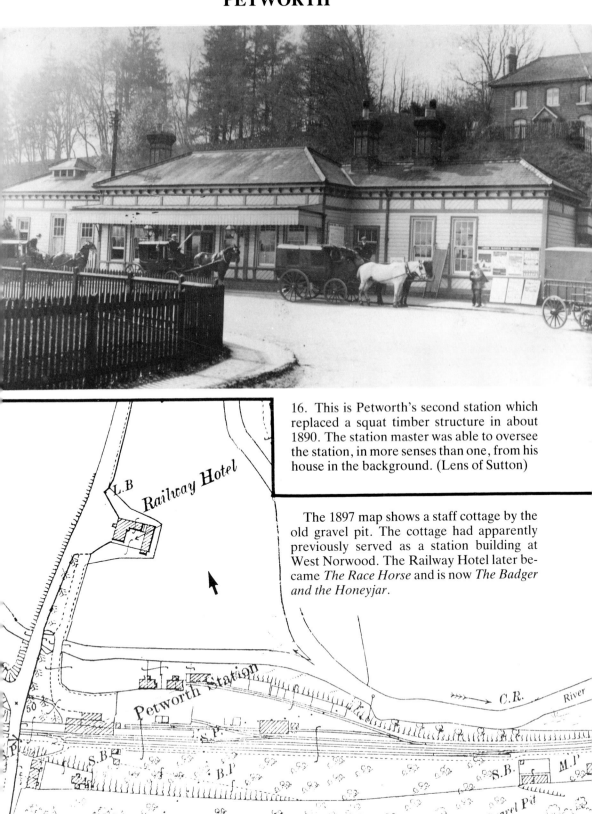

16. This is Petworth's second station which replaced a squat timber structure in about 1890. The station master was able to oversee the station, in more senses than one, from his house in the background. (Lens of Sutton)

The 1897 map shows a staff cottage by the old gravel pit. The cottage had apparently previously served as a station building at West Norwood. The Railway Hotel later became *The Race Horse* and is now *The Badger and the Honeyjar*.

17. A loop was provided but it was for the use of goods trains only. Another photograph from around 1900 reveals that generous canopies were provided on both sides of the building. (R. Resch collection)

18. The proximity of the River Rother is clear from this 1923 signal post view of the layout. A locomotive shed was provided here when the station was a terminus and it was later removed to Hayling Island station. (Late E. Wallis)

19. Management often encourage their staff "to get out into the field". Here a representative of the SR assists with the loading of kale onto the company's lorry at Soanes Farm, in March 1931. Look for the oversize overcoat and the crooked crank handle. (G. Garland)

22. Surrounded by official notices and excursion handbills, Station Master Cripps receives a presentation desk on 12th April 1949. Sometime after closure these premises were used for the manufacture of small wooden elephants. (G. Garland collection)

20. The station was inconveniently situated over two miles south of the town. In 1930 it was evidently thought necessary to indicate in large letters that there was a station named after the town. By then, buses were running conveniently to the centres of adjacent towns. (Mrs M. Greenfield collection)

21. A 1939 view from the main road shows the roofs of the signal box and station master's house with three staff cottages in the foreground. The latter suffered blast damage during WWII, when a bomb exploded just west of the bridge.
(Mrs M. Greenfield collection)

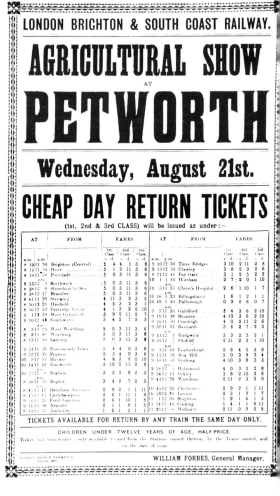

LONDON BRIGHTON & SOUTH COAST RAILWAY.

AGRICULTURAL SHOW
AT
PETWORTH
Wednesday, August 21st.
CHEAP DAY RETURN TICKETS
(1st, 2nd & 3rd CLASS) will be issued as under :—

TICKETS AVAILABLE FOR RETURN BY ANY TRAIN THE SAME DAY ONLY.

CHILDREN UNDER TWELVE YEARS OF AGE, HALF PRICE.

Tickets not transferable; only available to and from the Stations named thereon, by the Trains named, and on the date of issue.

WILLIAM FORBES, General Manager.

1907 handbill

23. On 14th April 1954, class E4 0–6–2T no. 32464 wheezes towards the buffer stops while shunting the yard. The station master's 'observation' house is on the skyline. On the smokebox is chalked *Genevieve* – the name of a veteran car that featured in a film popular at that time. (P. Hay)

25. A Pulborough bound train stands opposite the Saxby & Farmer designed signal box
on the last day of public passenger services.
The box remained in use for nearly two years
more, closing on 22nd December 1957.
Another bomb during WWII damaged the
London end of the platform. (S.C. Nash)

24. In 1932, both ends of the platform
canopy were removed. Over twenty years
later, we see two coaches about to be propelled to Midhurst, while shunting proceeds in
the yard. The foot crossing in the foreground
was for staff from the nearby dwellings.
(D. Cullum collection)

26. Circus elephants arrived by rail in September 1959. It was a long walk to the town –
hence the bicycle lamp on the forehead of the
larger animal. More common livestock
included horses to and from Lavington Stud
Farm and sheep brought from Romney
Marsh for winter grazing in the area.
(G. Garland collection)

27. A photograph taken on 16th October 1961 shows that the loop had gone by then (it had been lifted in 1957) and that, in the absence of a signal box, the ground frame had to be unlocked before use. The guard can be seen parting the train, leaving the wagons from Midhurst in the platform during shunting procedures. It was simpler to take wagons for Petworth via Midhurst!
(D. Fereday Glenn)

→

28. Diesel class 08 locomotives worked out to Petworth in the final months of freight operation, until they ceased on 20th May 1966. Goods inward included domestic coal and bulk grain wagons bringing Canadian wheat to Gwillim's nearby Coultershaw flour mills, which were powered by water turbines. Hence the grain storage and loading equipment visible in the picture.
(G. Garland collection)

SOUTHERN RAILWAY.
This half available on the
DATE of issue ONLY.

Selham
TO
PETWORTH

8d. THIRD CLASS. FARE

0029

→

29. By 1972, the coal merchant had moved into the former carriage drive. After years of neglect and after having been involved with real elephants and toy elephants, the station has been tastefully converted into a desirable residence. (A.J. Hoskins)

SELHAM

30. Like Fittleworth, Selham station came into use some time after the line opened. Traffic commenced here on 1st July 1872. This 1923 westward view emphasises its rural location, traffic being generated from the wide surrounding agricultural area. (Late E. Wallis)

The 1912 map indicates the position of the signal box (S.B.). "Three" is part of the name of the *Three Moles Inn*, a name which remains unchanged today.

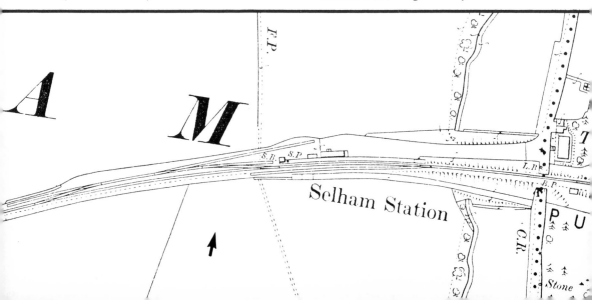

31. All stations on the route handled a substantial milk traffic – these churns held 17 gallons and weighed nearly 2cwt when full. Local passenger traffic was light, as the population of the village only rose from 48 in 1894 to 65 in 1938. (G. Garland collection)

32. Looking east, we see the wooden platform surface (which was kind to milk churns); the small cattle dock (which had an exclusive road approach) and the roof of the *Three Moles*. (Pamlin Prints)

33. With the abolition of the signal box in 1933, two ground frames had to be provided – one for the goods yard and this one for the dock siding. The gradient post emphasises the undulating nature of the route. (D. Cullum)

35. After shunting at Selham, class E4 0–6–2T no. 32469 proceeds towards Pulborough on 21st December 1960. The yard, which was notable for the amount of chestnut fencing despatched (for example, 750 tons in 1937), closed in May 1963.
(D. Fereday Glenn)

34. The semi-clad fireman cools off as his M7 (no. 30481) accelerates towards Petworth. The well maintained cattle road on the left is now totally overgrown and impassable.
(Lens of Sutton)

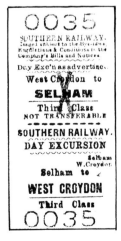

36. The last passenger working to Midhurst was an enthusiasts' special composed of smartly turned out Bulleid designed stock, including a buffet car. Q class no. 30530 passes the west ground frame on 18th October 1964, a memorable but sad day for many. (S.C. Nash)

About half way between Selham and Midhurst tunnel the line crossed a public road on an overbridge near South Ambersham. The 1912 edition shows that sufficient land was fenced off for the erection of a station and that a drive way was constructed but no such development took place.

3rd · SINGLE
Midhurst to
SELHAM
(8) 3½d.   FARE   3½d. (8)
FOR CONDITIONS SEE OVER
0104   6104

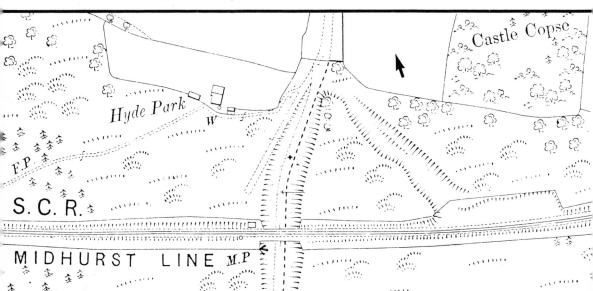

37. In addition to competition from South-down buses running along the main road, the SR suffered from Hants & Sussex vehicles mopping up passengers from the Down-foot villages. Their success required the introduction of Dennis Lance double deckers, when the Midhurst - Graffham route was extended to Petworth in 1945. The company painted white lines on the road, to help drivers negotiate the bridge at Ambersham Common, which was demolished in about 1970. (Late C. Klapper)

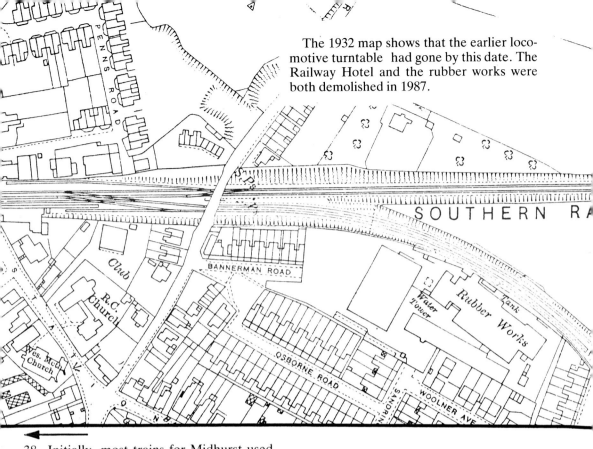

The 1932 map shows that the earlier locomotive turntable had gone by this date. The Railway Hotel and the rubber works were both demolished in 1987.

38. Initially, most trains for Midhurst used the loop line on the left but eventually a bay platform was provided on the down side, beyond the level crossing gates in the distance. The buildings have changed little since this photograph was taken in 1911. (British Rail)

39. From 1919 until 1937, many Midhurst services used the main platforms on Sundays, as the trains ran to and from Portsmouth. In the background are the South Downs, which are pierced by a tunnel near Butser Hill. (Lens of Sutton)

40. The Midhurst platform was convenient for the Operating Department but not popular with passengers on wet days. On the left is the SCATS siding and two coaches stand in the South Eastern Farmers' siding leading to the ITS Rubber Works. This 1928 photograph shows the up starting signal on the down main platform. (Late E. Wallis)

Other maps and photographs of this station appear in our *Branch Lines to Midhurst* and *Woking to Portsmouth* albums.

41. The staff pose on the final day of operation – 5th February 1955. Station Master Vaus, gloves in hand; Guard Horwood, flag in hand and Foreman Tupper, with collar pinned. (C. White)

42. Class M7 no. 30028 speeds off to Midhurst on the penultimate day of operation as a pedestrian from North Road waits to cross the line. Users of this footpath had to climb over the disused embankment until it was cut through in 1985. The end of ITS siding is on the left. (A. Hemans collection)

43. Half way between Petersfield and Rogate, near Ryefield Farm, class M7 no. 26 left the rails while hauling the 10.22 am to Midhurst on 16th June 1937. None of the three passengers were injured and, following an inquiry, the ganger was reduced to the rank of a lengthman for failing to align and level the track correctly and for failing to report speeding drivers on other occasions. (C. White collection)

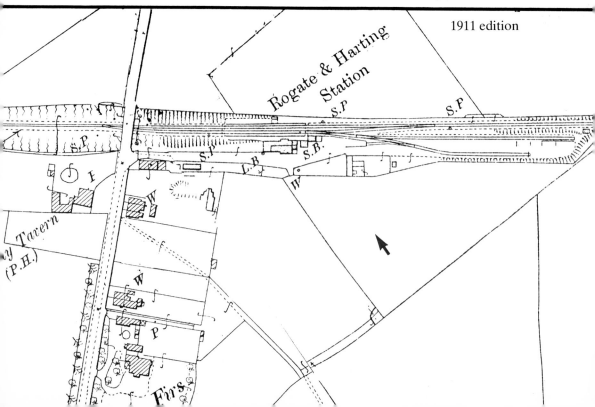

44. Known variously as Rogate for Harting and Rogate & Harting, the station was 1½ miles from each place, in the village of Nyewood. All three stations on this LSWR branch were originally identical. The signal box, in this 1954 view, seems neglected but it had only served as a ground frame since 1932. (D. Cullum)

L. & S. W. R. (862B)

MILK. From ROGATE & HARTING

TO

CLAPHAM JC.

45. Class M7 no. 30028 arrives from Petersfield on 14th August 1954. In the background is the Nyewood brickworks siding which was not shown on the 1911 map, as it was not laid until the works was moved to a later, more northerly, location. (D. Cullum)

46. The photographer stands on the long-disused down platform as mineral wagons loaded with sugar beet approach on 6th November 1954. The wooden panels behind the seats were a late addition to the waiting area. Your author converted the building into a factory for Mitchell Mouldings Ltd in 1968, for the production of acrylic castings. (R.C. Riley)

47. Class E5X nos. 32570 and 32576 return to Horsham depot on 6th February 1955 after having worked "The Hampshireman" to Petersfield. This was the last passenger carrying train to run west of Midhurst. On the extreme left is a small wooden goods shed in which the milk churn label, illustrated here, was found in 1969. (S.C. Nash)

SOUTHERN RAILWAY.
Issued subject to the Bye-laws, Regulations & Conditions in the Company's Bills and Notices.
Midhurst to
Midhurst
Portsmouth & S'sea
PORTSMOUTH & SOUTHSEA
THIRD CLASS
Fare 4/5
NOT TRANSFERABLE.
739

ELSTED

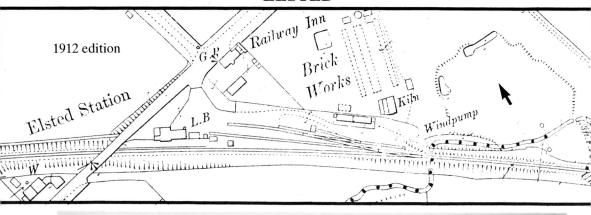

1912 edition

←———

48. The station was over a mile north of the village and changed little during its 91 year life. Unusually, this train bears neither head code nor tail light and the photographer did not record the details. (D. Cullum collection)

50. No. 30050 is seen propelling two coaches west on 14th April 1954 with the wind pump visible under the bridge and the Railway Inn to its left. The latter has recently been renamed *Ballards* and claims to be Britain's smallest brewery. (P. Hay)

←———

49. Class M7 no. 30328, displaying both head code and tail light, blows off as she waits to propel the single coach to Petersfield in April 1953. The building still stands although heavily disguised as part of a farm tractor reconditioning business. (S.C. Nash)

51. The demolition contractor's crane stands by the ground frame, as men prepare to fell the wind pump. The District Engineer made an inspection of the line on 4th October 1956, travelling on a Matisa tamping machine from Petersfield. (A. Hall)

3. Chichester towards Midhurst

CHICHESTER

52. By the time the first train arrived at Chichester in 1846, Goodwood Races were already well established. This later photograph shows racegoers leaving the station, at the beginning of their journey of over four miles to the course. Both signal boxes are visible as is a belfry on the down side buildings. The footbridge had not been erected and fields extend beyond the station. (Author's collection)

L. B. & S. L. & S. W. & Great Western Rys
Available for 2 days including date of issue
CHICHESTER TO
BRISTOL
Via Havant, Salisbury & G. W. Ry.
8s 9½d. **THIRD CLASS.** 8s. 9½d.
The connection of trains not guaranteed.
Not transferable. Issued subject to the
Conditions in the Time Tables of the respective
Co.s over whose lines ticket is available.

2755

53. The first station buildings were completed in about 1847 and remained in use for 110 years until replaced by the present structure – one of BR's top eight prestige stations. Top-hatted Station Master Harold Bridger poses with his staff near the up side entrance, in about 1900. (L.C.G. Holden collection)

54. Bay platforms were provided at the west end of the station, on both sides. This is the up side, from which most Midhurst services departed. Class D1 0–4–2T no.225 was scrapped in 1925 and this area was filled in to form a car park in 1986. (Lens of Sutton)

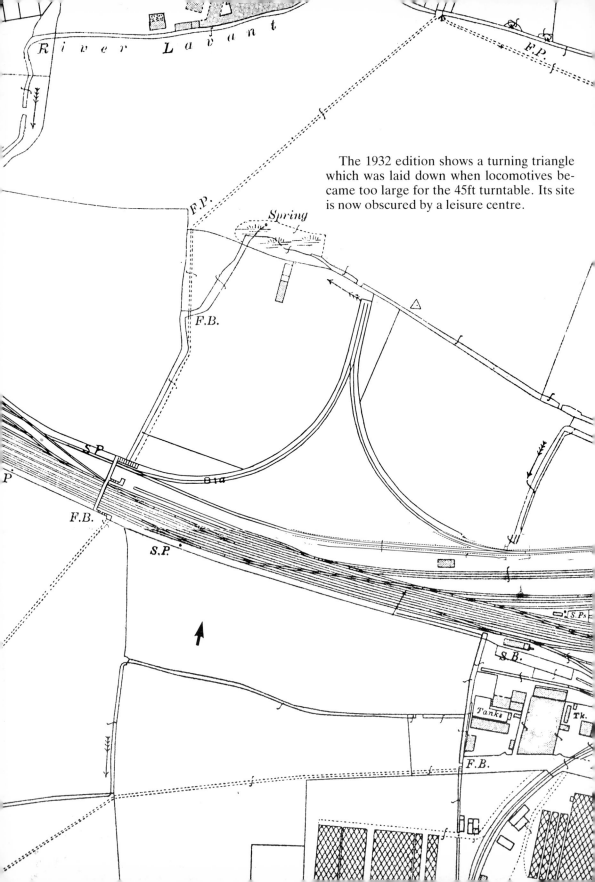

The 1932 edition shows a turning triangle which was laid down when locomotives became too large for the 45ft turntable. Its site is now obscured by a leisure centre.

River Lavant

F.P.

F.P.

Spring

F.B.

S.P.

P

F.B.

S.P.

S.Ps

S.B.

Tanks

Tk.

F.B.

55. A view from the lengthy footbridge includes part of the triangle; a class Q1 0–6–0 and class E4 no. 2501 entering the up reception road, which is still electrified for half its length. The down sidings, most of the up ones and both bay lines have been removed. (C.R.L. Coles)

For further photographs and maps of Chichester see:
Branch Lines to Midhurst
Branch Line to Selsey
Worthing to Chichester
Chichester to Portsmouth

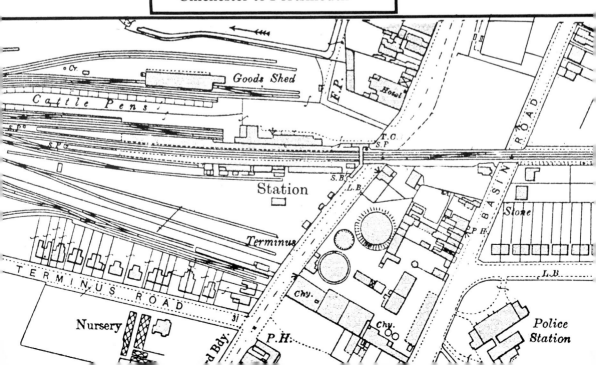

FISHBOURNE CROSSING

56. The Midhurst line, on the right, had its own independent single line parallel to the main lines for ¾ mile to Chichester station. Note the double arm branch signal and a train approaching from Portsmouth. (Lens of Sutton)

57. On 7th February 1954, the connection in front of no. 73134 came into use, the third track over the level crossing was soon removed and shorter gates fitted. The photograph was taken on 3rd June 1981 of what was believed to be the last gravel train from Lavant. However, operation recommenced in September 1983, having initially started in 1972. (D. Dornom)

58. Looking towards Chichester from the signal box steps on 29th May 1987, we see the new road bridge under construction which will render the crossing obsolete. The box was still operating mechanical equipment and had 21 levers plus two spares.
(V. Mitchell)

59. Your authors arranged for a number of events to take place on 11th July 1981, to celebrate the centenary of the opening of the line. This is an Eastleigh based DEMU which was operated by the local Woking Homes Committee that day, viewed from Brandy Hole Lane Bridge. (J. Petley)

60. 1½ miles north of the junction, a passing loop was laid in 1972 to enable the locomotive to run round the empty gravel train before propelling it ½ mile north for loading. Here we look south from the foot crossing at Plainwood Close to Brandy Hole Lane Bridge. (V. Mitchell)

61. Gravel is transported over ½ mile by conveyor belt before being loaded into special 90-ton hopper wagons for transport to the washing and grading plant at Drayton, two miles east of Chichester. No. 73134 *Woking Homes*, in its latest livery, eases the heavy train forward as it is being loaded in stages, on 22nd September 1986. (V. Mitchell)

LAVANT

62. Looking north under the main road bridge, it is clear that the buildings were on three different levels with additional steps leading down to the platform externally. A Terrier 0–6–0T appears to be hauling a vehicle of a type better seen in picture no.12 in *Branch Line to Hayling*. (Lens of Sutton)

→

64. The station house and offices have changed little since this photograph was taken in 1957. The local authority acquired the property and have erected dwellings in the yard but have not yet implemented plans to adapt the buildings for the elderly. (R.A. Holder)

63. No sidings were provided initially but an additional track was eventually laid under the bridges to a gravel pit, near the Chichester Road. A run round loop on it, north of the Westbridge Path crossing, gave triple track for a short way. (Lens of Sutton)

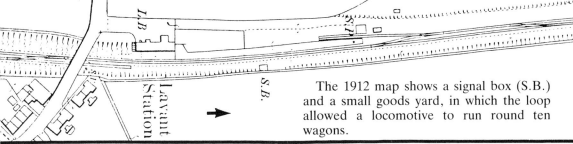

The 1912 map shows a signal box (S.B.) and a small goods yard, in which the loop allowed a locomotive to run round ten wagons.

1922 Appendix to the service timetable.

Lavant.—Passenger Trains running in opposite directions must not cross or pass each other at this Station. A Goods or Ballast Train, or Engine, may shunt for a Passenger Train to pass, but permission must not be given either to Chichester or Singleton Stations for a Staff to be drawn until the Goods or Ballast Train, or Engine has been shunted clear of the Main Line.

The Station Master will be held personally responsible for seeing that the Goods Train, Ballast Train or Light Engine has been shunted clear of the Main Line before the Train Staff is given up to the Signalman.

Lavant: Government Siding.—This Siding is connected with the Single Line between Lavant and Singleton about ¼ mile north of Lavant Station. The points are worked from a ground frame controlled by Annett's Patent Lock, the key of which is fixed to the Electric Train Staff for the Section between Lavant and Singleton. The ground frame cannot be used unless the key is in the lock and the key cannot be withdrawn until the points are reset to their normal position. A gate is provided across the entrance to the siding, the key of which is kept in Lavant Signal Box. Disc Signals govern movements to and from the Siding.

The siding is under the control of the Station Master at Lavant Station. All Trucks for the siding must be invoiced and worked to Lavant Station, thence to the siding by Up Goods Trains as arranged by the Station Master.

Up Trains calling at the siding must run on from there to Singleton Station.

Lavant: Gravel Pit Siding.—When propelling Trucks to the Gravel Pit Siding at Lavant, if a Brake Van is not the leading vehicle all Truck Brake Levers must be pinned down. If the number of Trucks provided with pins is insufficient to securely hold them, a Sprag must be used in the leading Truck, and when there are more than ten Trucks two Sprags must be used. Twenty-five Trucks must be the maximum number propelled.

65. A number of important changes took place in 1953, when Lavant became the railhead and loading point for sugar beet from a wide area. The open part of the platform was resurfaced with concrete to facilitate this and a long run round loop was laid. Both can be seen in this picture of class C2X 0–6–0 no. 32550 shunting beet on 15th October 1955. (S.C. Nash)

66. Another view of the same event shows the scotch block on the main line and the canopy, which was later removed by the Bluebell Railway for re-use at Horsted Keynes. No. 32550 is standing on the reception road, to which the self-acting points at the south of the station were always set. (S.C. Nash)

67. Empty mineral wagons pass under the substantial footbridge on 3rd October 1965, soon to be filled with part of the vast tonnage of sugar beet loaded here every autumn, until 1969. Curiously this traffic was classified by BR as "minerals other than coal".
(R.A. Holder)

68. Small amounts of coal continued to be received at Lavant and here we see the last *regular* freight train, on 3rd August 1968. Sugar beet was loaded in the autumn of 1969, official closure being in January 1970.
(J.A.M. Vaughan)

69. One of the locomotives used by the contractor (T. Oliver of Horsham) was *Fred*, a Manning Wardle Type E 0–4–0ST which had a wheelbase of only 4′9″. Note the extra pair of dumb wooden buffers used by the small earth-moving wagons.
(Late E. Wallis collection)

71. By 1922, Singleton South Box was only staffed on alternate Wednesdays and race days. The brick base supporting the locomotive water tank, on the left, can still be seen from West Dean sports field.
(Lens of Sutton)

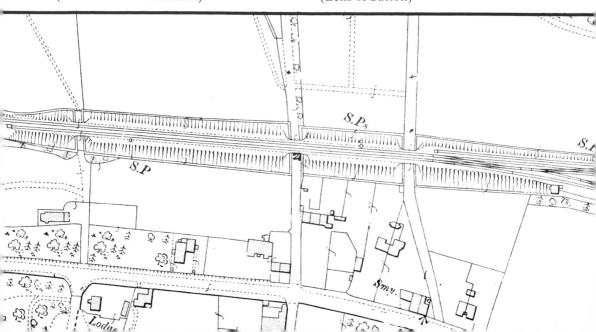

70. The station is nearly complete but there are as yet no platform canopies and no canopy linking the subway (on the left) with the station entrance. An avenue of trees was planted which now completely bridge the approach road. The very generous facilities provided were only fully used during the few days of the annual Goodwood Races. (Late E. Wallis collection)

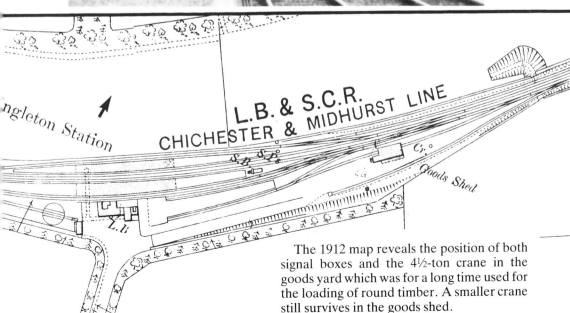

ngleton Station

L.B. & S.C.R.
CHICHESTER & MIDHURST LINE

Goods Shed

L.B

The 1912 map reveals the position of both signal boxes and the 4½-ton crane in the goods yard which was for a long time used for the loading of round timber. A smaller crane still survives in the goods shed.

72. Up to fourteen 20-coach trains could be stabled in the sidings, the total length of which was over ¾ mile. This busy scene is viewed from North Box. Horse box traffic would add to the congestion in the sidings, which would be little used for the rest of the year. (Lens of Sutton)

73. At the end of the nineteenth century the Prince of Wales used the elegant station when visiting the nearby West Dean Park, but on race days it seems that the station was mainly used by third class passengers who would walk up the steep hill to the course. The accompanying handbill shows that other racegoers used Drayton or Chichester stations, from where road transport could negotiate the more gentle slope to the grandstands. (Lens of Sutton)

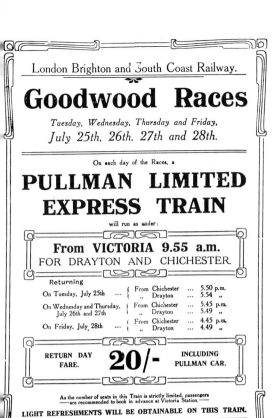

74. Tom Reeves operated a competitive road service not only carting goods but also conveying passengers to Chichester for 6d (2½p). The discomfort of unsprung wheels on flint roads could be compensated by door to door service. (A. Hemans collection)

75. Mr. W.G. Dowle, a local farmer, started to increase the competition for passengers by operating a red Model T Ford. Travellers would be picked up anywhere along the road, except outside the railway stations. Thus rail-users had to be suitably humiliated as the bus passed by. The service was absorbed by Southdown, with whom the SR made arrangements for the carriage of passengers after 1935. (Author's collection)

76. The panorama north and the next mile of the route offered superb views of the heart of the South Downs, but the subsequent two miles were in cutting or tunnel. Scheduled services normally passed on the centre tracks except school trains, which used the outer platform faces to reduce the incidence of juvenile warfare.
(E.R. Lacey/R.C. Riley collection)

78. On the left is one of the largest gentleman's toilet blocks ever built for a country station. The 46ft turntable was on the bank above it. In 1972, the Paget Bros. established a vineyard on the hillside west of the platforms. In 1987, it was still possible to walk through the subway to see the vines and to sample the end product in the former booking hall. (Lens of Sutton)

This ticket is of particular interest as it appears to be for a groom travelling in a horse box. No through regular passenger services operated over the East London Railway in the post grouping era and the statement on the ticket that *the connection of trains is not guaranteed* implies that there were often delays when horse boxes were being transferred from the end of one passenger train to another.

SOUTHERN. E. L. & L. & N. E. RYS.
Available for 3 Days including date of issue.

0166

SINGLETON TO

NEWMARKET

Via New X Gate, E. L. RY. & Bishopsgate.

16/10 **THIRD CLASS.** Fare 16/10

The connection of trains not guaranteed.
Not transferable. Issued subject to the
Conditions in the TimeTables of the respective
Co's over whose lines this ticket is available.

0166

77. The scene of dereliction in September 1953, a few weeks after goods services ceased, does not include the two remaining tracks as they were either side of the far platform. The canopies were demolished in May 1956. In the final years, the goods office was staffed part-time and was entered by the double doors on the right. The area has subsequently been used for refurbishing ex-service lorries for use as lime spreaders, gritters, etc. (S.C. Nash)

79. With a population of under 500, the village did not generate much passenger traffic and by 1932 the station ceased to be manned. Thereafter only complete wagon loads of goods were received and the 16-lever signal box only functioned as a ground frame. (E.R. Lacey collection)

80. From November 1951 until closure in August 1953, Cocking was the northern terminus of the line which was then worked without signalling on the "one engine in steam" system. Cocking Tunnel is in the distance – the land in between it and the station was built up from the excavated spoil. (Lens of Sutton) ➤

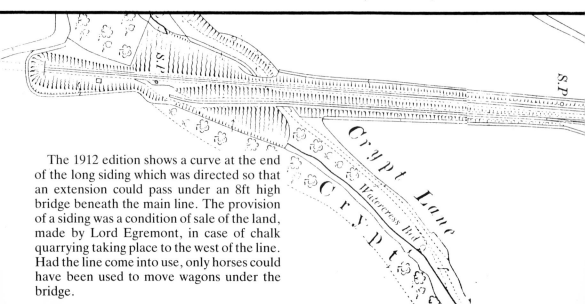

The 1912 edition shows a curve at the end of the long siding which was directed so that an extension could pass under an 8ft high bridge beneath the main line. The provision of a siding was a condition of sale of the land, made by Lord Egremont, in case of chalk quarrying taking place to the west of the line. Had the line come into use, only horses could have been used to move wagons under the bridge.

S.P.

S.B.

S.P.

Cocking Sta

Recto

81. The lavish ornamentation and floral patterns in the plasterwork were typical of the 1880 stations from Lavant to Midhurst. When photographed in 1958, the house was still occupied, it having been built on two rows of subterranean arches. (H.C. Casserley)

82. The building now makes a desirable residence, having had the booking office area doubled in height and the tile-hanging removed from the south elevation. (P. Clark collection)

83. On 9th September 1904, while working the 3 pm goods train from Midhurst to Singleton and back, D class no. 239 *Patcham* mysteriously left the rails on the return journey, having just passed over Park Lane bridge, which is opposite the Heyshott turning. The crew was uninjured but a wagon, a van and the guards van were badly damaged. (Lens of Sutton)

84. Two days later the steam cranes from Brighton and New Cross attended to the re-railing with some difficulty. Trains ran to either side of the obstruction and passengers walked past the spectacle. (E. Jackson collection)

85. A small stream, which feeds South Pond, passed under the line in a culvert about ½ mile south of Midhurst station, at the end of the present Holmbush Industrial Estate. On 19th November 1951, the culvert became blocked and the embankment was washed away by the impounded water. The crew of the morning up goods train jumped for their lives and the firebox of class C2X no. 32522 continued to be fed by coal from the leading wagon for the next few days. This is the scene on 14th February 1952, after the embankment had been cut away from behind the tender.
(British Rail)

86. On 25th February 1952, a locomotive, in the background, was ready to apply force through the Kelbus tackle on the track to haul no. 32522 up the temporary way. Its coupling rods rest in the stream while some odd shaped rails lie on the cut-back bank. The locomotive was eventually repaired and gave several years more service.
(British Rail)

4. Midhurst

MIDHURST LBSCR

87. An artist's impression of the LBSCR terminus, dated 1876, portrays that company's contemporary rolling stock fairly well, but the LSWR's station in the background is less accurate. (D. Cullum collection)

88. The second LBSCR station was opened with the Chichester line on 11th July 1881 and was ¼ mile east of its predecessor. This view from the Petworth end was taken just prior to the opening. (Chichester Reference Library)

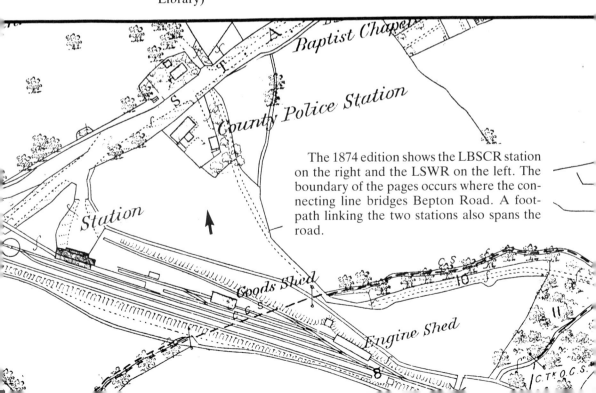

The 1874 edition shows the LBSCR station on the right and the LSWR on the left. The boundary of the pages occurs where the connecting line bridges Bepton Road. A footpath linking the two stations also spans the road.

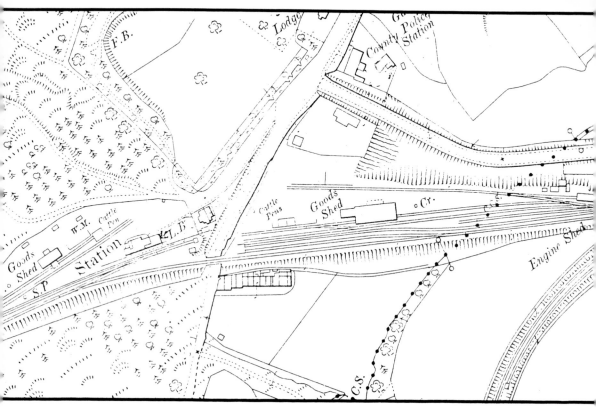

89. After 1881, passengers transferring from the LSWR to the new LBSCR station had the choice of walking along a rough track or up Station Road (now Bepton Road); along West Street; down the Chichester Road and into the station approach road. Eventually the two companies agreed to build a new road, 30ft wide with two footways. It is still known as New Road and was dedicated to public use in 1895 and adopted by Midhurst Rural District Council in 1899. (R. Resch collection)

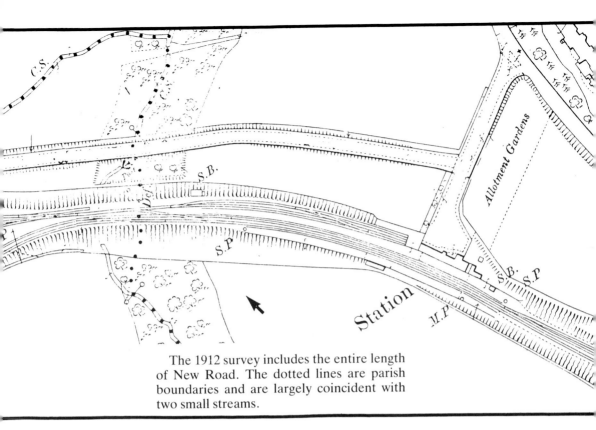

The 1912 survey includes the entire length of New Road. The dotted lines are parish boundaries and are largely coincident with two small streams.

90. Class D 0–4–2T no. 34 *Balham* stands in the up platform sometime before 1908, when she was renumbered 634. Midhurst South Box ceased to function after the SR rationali- sation in 1925, eventually being transformed into a peaceful station master's office, remote from the bustle of the station. (Lens of Sutton)

91. There was considerable bustle outside the station when King Edward VII transferred from his train to a coach to make the journey to the new Sanatorium which he officially opened on 13th June 1906. He would have had a shorter journey via Haslemere but maybe he had sentimental memories of journeys by train via Midhurst to week-end parties at West Dean. (C. White collection)

London Brighton and South Coast Railway.

EPSOM RACES

MAY 29th, 30th & 31st, & JUNE 1st.

THE MID-SUSSEX AND DORKING ROUTE

IS THE

ONLY DIRECT ROUTE

FROM

THE ISLE OF WIGHT

IN CONNECTION WITH THE THROUGH TRAINS RUN BETWEEN

PORTSMOUTH AND EPSOM

WITHOUT CHANGE OF CARRIAGE.

ON EACH OF THE ABOVE RACE DAYS

Cheap Return Tickets

(1st and 2nd Class) will be issued as under:-

A.M.	FROM	RETURN FARES.				Returning from EPSOM
		1st CLASS		2nd CLASS.		
		s.	D.	s.	D.	
9 50	Portsmouth Harbour	16	0	10	6	the same or following day by any Train, and those issued on Friday, June 1st, will be available to return from London Bridge or Victoria by any Train on Saturday, June 2nd.
9 55	Portsmouth Town					
9 57	Fratton & Southsea	15	0	10	0	
10 9	Havant					
9 15	Midhurst	12	0	8	0	Returning from EPSOM TOWN at 5.30 or 7.55 p.m. These Tickets will also be available to return by any Train the following day.
9 23	Selham	11	2	8	0	
9 30	Petworth	10	6	8	0	
9 37	Fittleworth	9	11	7	8	

On DERBY DAY

AN ADDITIONAL SPECIAL FAST TRAIN

AT THE ABOVE CHEAP FARES WILL ALSO

Leave PORTSMOUTH HARBOUR 8.55 a.m.

PORTSMOUTH TOWN ... 9.0 a.m. | FRATTON & SOUTHSEA ... 9.2. a.m.

HAVANT ... 9.14 a.m.

This Special Fast Train will Return from Epsom Town at 6.25 p.m.

London Bridge Terminus, May, 1906.   WILLIAM FORBES, General Manager.

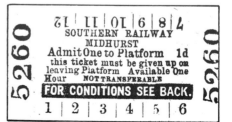

MIDHURST (LSWR)

South Western Midhurst

92. Initially, the terminal building was similar to those at Elsted and Rogate but in 1881 this handsome and useful canopy was added. Presumably, the opening of the rivals' new luxurious station prompted this.
(Lens of Sutton)

93. A postcard view from the Common shows that two staff cottages were provided, to the left of the station. They remain in use today. A fourth bedroom was added to the station house in 1898, not a fifth as misprinted in our *Midhurst Town - Then & Now*.
(Lens of Sutton)

94. Looking west in November 1923, we see the main line from Petersfield to the left of the signal box and the Midhurst Whites brickworks behind it. The box and the station closed on 4th April 1925, after which all trains ran into the bay of the former LBSCR station. (Late E. Wallis)

After some years of dereliction, the station house was renovated for use as offices. In 1987, it was substantially extended by Redgrove & Kemp (civil and structural consulting engineers) for use as their headquarters.

MIDHURST (SR)

95. A D class 0–4–2T creeps round the sharp curve with a train from Chichester, in about 1930. To the right of the two signals are roofs of the former LSWR station, LBSCR goods shed and engine shed. The latter ceased to be used regularly after 1st December 1921. Note that Petersfield trains were given a straight run into the bay platform, although it was 44 years before they could use it. (Lens of Sutton)

96. Looking west from near the tunnel mouth at about the same time, the features of the previous photograph are visible in the distance. In the foreground is the sand pit of Hall & Co., the face of which now gives rise to a steep incline in a residential road – The Fairway. The line to Petworth is nearest the camera. (Lens of Sutton)

97. Facing east in the former LSWR goods yard, it is clear that the track was moved away from the platform when the tracks were repositioned in 1925 to allow through running. The yard and the private sidings to Midhurst Whites remained in use however. (R. Shepherd)

98. A view west confirms this and also shows the goods yard crane and stacks of white bricks. The bricks were made from lime, produced at Cocking, and sand brought into the works on a 2'6" gauge railway from a nearby pit. Production ceased in 1986. Timber is being removed from that part of the platform on which milk churns had once been handled. (R. Shepherd)

99. As both maps show, the LSWR engine shed was remote from the station. Its integral water tank is visible but the turntable had gone when photographed, not long before closure, in 1937. (R. Shepherd)

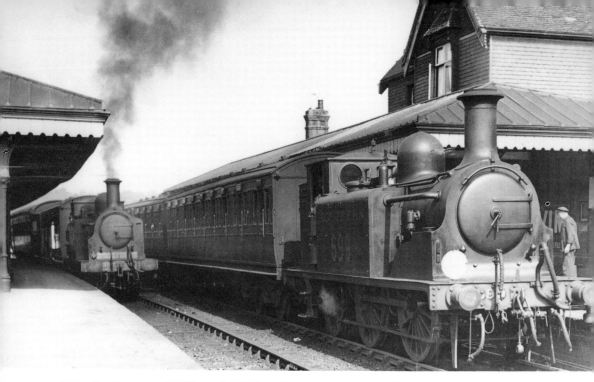

100. D class nos. B699 and B357 wait at Midhurst's second LBSCR station, on 30th August 1930. The only other passing places for passenger trains on the three lines at that time were Singleton and Rogate. Engines were invariably at the Pulborough end of trains in latter years. (H.C. Casserley)

101. The Nyewood Brickworks Garrett steam lorry was often hired by Midhurst Whites to move coal from the former LBSCR goods yard to their works, although it had its own siding! This irony is explained by the fact that the SR was still operating pre-grouping tarrifs and would have charged more for Kent coal to be brought by an LSWR route. Stent was a Midhurst coal merchant – one of his own wagons is visible. (C. White collection)

102. The penultimate passenger train to Chichester emerges from Midhurst tunnel on 5th July 1935 and clatters past the sand pit crane. Dangerous icicles sometimes formed in this 276 yard long bore. (Dr. I.C. Allen)

1910 advertisement.

MIDHURST (BR)

103. A train from Petersfield passes the ex-LSWR station on 1st December 1951, while washing on the line indicates that the house was still occupied. By then, the original canopy had gone and the bedroom had been slate hung, to reduce water penetration. (R.C. Riley)

104. Class M7 no. 30108 sets off for Petersfield, on the same day. The 47-lever signal box was not a popular place to work – its southward aspect made it like a greenhouse in summer and its numerous draughty sliding windows made it resemble a barn in winter. (R.C. Riley)

SOUTHERN RAILWAY.
Admit ONE MOTOR CAR
to be Parked
in the Station Approach at
MIDHURST
CHARGE 1/-
FOR CONDITIONS SEE BACK.

0321

0321

105. This June 1952 photograph is included to emphasise the generous lengths of the canopies. No wonder the LSWR thought that they should add one to their station! A curious feature was the up platform nameboard at right angles to the track. (D. Clayton)

106. A tapered wooden LBSCR signal post was still in use when the 5.41pm from Pulborough arrived on 25th April 1953. Class M7 no. 30328 was propelling. Unlike the overbridges and tunnels on the Chichester route, Midhurst tunnel was built for a single track only. (S.C. Nash)

BRITISH RAILWAYS (S)
This ticket is issued subject to the Bye-laws, Regulations and Conditions contained in the Publications and Notices of and applicable to the Railway Executive.
Available on Day of issue ONLY.
Midhurst to
HORSHAM
THIRD CLASS
Issued in exchange for Return Ticket issued by Southdown Motor Services Limited, upon payment of the supplementary charge of 8/3
NOT TRANSFERABLE.

107. No. 30110 propels a lightweight LBSCR driving trailer west on 14th April 1954, as we have a chance to examine the runs of point rodding necessary to work a simple country junction safely. The junction of New Road and Station Approach is to be seen on the left; the two chestnut trees survive today. (P. Hay)

108. The sky darkens as sister M7 no. 30028 accelerates east, on the same day. Few station masters would have had sliding windows on their office. The line in the foreground led to a sand drag, which was used on one occasion by several empty wagons that ran away from Cocking tunnel. They had been stored there prior to D-Day and had been subjected to a rough shunt. (D. Cullum)

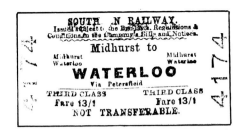

← 109. The first of four photographs dated 6th November 1954 was taken from the former LSWR terminus and shows the bridge over Bepton Road (which had been rebuilt in 1925) together with the former LBSCR goods shed. (R.C. Riley)

← 110. On the left is the Chichester line up home signal, which had been almost unused for three years. To the right of Q class no. 30545 is the capacious locomotive water tank, which remained in use to the end of freight services. (R.C. Riley)

111. The camera was turned through 180° to reveal the infamous leaning signal box of Midhurst. It appears that the weight of the lever frame had caused it to settle into the sandy embankment. The latter had made the first engine shed sink unevenly. (R.C. Riley)

112. A photograph from the signal box shows no. 30545 to have completed its shunting and also reveals the crossover in the Petersfield bay. Nearby is the dock which once served to unload hundreds of polo ponies for Cowdray Park every summer. Beyond it is parked a bus of the Aldershot & District Traction Co, which then operated a half-hourly service to Haslemere station, giving residents their quickest route to London. (R.C. Riley)

113. Driver Brackpool, Fireman Penfold and Guard Shoebridge pose by class E5X no. 32576, on 3rd December 1954. Members of this class provided freight motive power on the line for many years. The power classification is shown – 2P/2F. (J. Scrace)

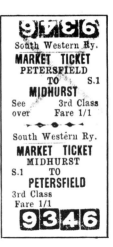

1910 Guide book.

114. Class E4s were also often used and one is seen here leaving with the last, but nominal, freight service to Petersfield on 4th February 1955. Its coal is stacked like bricks as it passes the brickworks' chimney and the remains of the locomotive shed. (S.C. Nash)

115. Pupils of Churcher's College, Petersfield, were allowed to make a farewell journey on the last day of operation, Saturday 5th February 1955. Another pupil's camera records somewhat spottily that the usual push-pull set no. 2 had been supplemented by an ex-LBSCR compartment coach. (D. Fereday Glenn)

116. The north facade was seldom photographed satisfactorily but at least it did not receive tile-hanging, like the east and south elevations did. Mr. Myers of Westminster designed the building and in the words of a contemporary report it included "a refreshment room, very handsomely fitted up, 18ft by 15ft, with ample accommodation in lavatories, closets, &c." (A. Hemans collection)

1937 working timetable

PETERSFIELD, MIDHURST AND PULBOROUGH.

Distance.	Distance from Midhurst.	WEEK-DAYS.				To Dorking N.				To Dorking N.		Mixed.			
				a.m.		a.m.		a.m.		a.m.		a.m.		a.m.	
M. C.	M. C.			arr.	dep.	arr.	dep.	arr	dep.	arr.	dep.	arr.	dep.	arr.	dep
...	...	PETERSFIELD		...	6 30	...	...	...	7 34	...	...	...	845	...	...
4 23	...	Rogate		6 38	6 39	...	...	7 42	7 43	...	...	853	856	...	...
6 22	...	Elsted		6 43	6 44	...	...	7 47	7 48	...	...	9 0	9 4	...	...
9 54	...	MIDHURST		6 51	...	...	725	7 55	...	...	9 5	911	...	...	10 10
...	3 29	Selham.........	S	...	...	732½	734½	...	...	912½	913	...	...	10 17½	10 18
...	5 68	Petworth		...	...	740	743	...	...	918½	921½	...	...	10 23½	10 24
...	8 0	Fittleworth ...		...	...	748½	749½	...	...	927	927½	...	...	10 29½	10 30
...	10 18	*Hardham Jct.*		...	...	753½	754	...	...	931½	932	...	...	10 34	10 34½
...	11 06	PULBOROUGH		...	...	756	8 0	...	...	934	947	...	...	10 36½	...

WEEK-DAYS.					B		D					
	a.m.		a.m.		a.m.		p.m.		p.m.		p.m.	
	arr.	dep.	arr.	dep.	arr.	dep.	arr.	dep.	arr.	dep.	arr.	de
PETERSFIELD	...	10 22	...	...	...	11 50	...	*12 1*	...	...	...	2
Rogate	10 30	10 31	...	...	11 58	11 59	*12 9*	*1210*	...	...	2 33	2
Elsted	10 35	10 36	...	...	12 3	12 4	*1214*	*1215*	...	...	2 38	2
MIDHURST	10 43	...	...	11 20	12 11	12 40	*1222*	*1240*	...	2 7	2 46	
Selham.........	...	...	11 27½	11 28	12 47½	12 48	*1247½*	*1248*	214½	215	...	
Petworth	...	...	11 33½	11 34	12 53½	12 54	*1253½*	*1254*	220½	221	...	
Fittleworth ...	...	...	11 39½	11 40	12 59½	1 0	*1259½*	*1 0*	226	227	...	
Hardham Jct.	...	...	11 44	11 44½	1 4	1 4½	*1 4*	*1 4½*	231	231½	...	
PULBOROUGH	...	...	11 46½	...	1 6½	...	*1 6½*	...	233½	...	...	

WEEK-DAYS.				To Horsham.				S.O.		S.X.		W.S.O.		To Horsham.	
		p.m.		p.m.		p.m.		p.m.		p.m.		p.m.		p.m.	
		arr.	dep.	arr.	dep.	arr.	dep.	arr.	dep.	arr.	dep.	arr.	dep.	arr.	dep.
PETERSFIELD		...	4 13	...	...	...	6 22	...	*7 25*	...	7 30	...	9 0	...	...
Rogate		4 21	4 22	...	...	6 30	6 31	*7 33*	*7 34*	7 38	7 39	9 8	9 9	...	...
Elsted		4 26	4 27	...	...	6 35	6 36	*7 38*	*7 39*	7 43	7 44	9 13	9 14	...	...
MIDHURST		4 34	...	...	4 38	6 43	...	*7 46*	*7 47*	7 51	8 0	9 21	...	...	9 58
Selham.........	S	...	...	4 45½	4 46½	...	...	*7 54½*	*7 55½*	8 7½	8 8	...	...	C	C
Petworth		...	...	4 52	4 54	...	...	*8 0½*	*8 1½*	8 13½	8 14½	...	...	1011½	1012½
Fittleworth ...		...	...	4 59½	5 1½	...	...	*8 5½*	*8 7½*	8 20	8 20½	...	...	10	18
Hardham Jct.		...	...	5 5½	5 6	...	...	*8 11½*	*8 12½*	8 24½	8 25	...	...	10 22	10 23
PULBOROUGH		...	...	5 8	5 10	...	...	*8 14½*	...	8 27	...	...	...	10 25	10 28

SUNDAYS.	To Three Bridges.								To L'hampto	
									Empty	
	a.m.		a.m.		p.m.		p.m.		p.m.	
	arr.	dep.	arr.	dep.	arr.	dep.	arr.	dep.	arr.	de
PETERSFIELD	...	6 20	...	10 49	...	4 12	...	7 5	...	...
Rogate	6 28	6 29	10 57	10 58	4 20	4 21	7 13	7 14	...	...
Elsted	6 33	6 34	11 2	11 3	4 25	4 26	7 18	7 19	...	...
MIDHURST	6 41	6 50	11 10	...	4 33	4 50	7 26	...	...	9 4
Selham.........	6 57½	7 1½	...	...	4 57½	5 0½	July 5th			9 52½
Petworth	7 7	7 10	...	...	5 6	5 8	to		9 58	9 5
Fittleworth ...	7 15½	7 18½	...	...	5 13½	5 14½	Sept. 27th		10	3
Hardham Jct.	7 22½	7 23	...	...	5 18½	5 19	only.		10 7	10
PULBOROUGH	7 25	7 28	...	...	5 21	...	...	...	...	...

a—Depart 12.39 p.m. on Saturdays.

B—Mondays to Fridays, July 6th to September 25th, daily commencing September 28th.

C—Calls at Selham on Saturdays only at 10.5½-10.6½ p.m.

D—Saturdays, July 11th to September 26th only.

LONDON PETERSFIELD, MIDHURST, PULBOROUGH, and LONDON
Third class only between Petersfield and Pulborough

	Down				Week Days												Sundays				
Miles		mrn	mrn	mrn	mrn	mrn	aft	aft			aft	aft	aft	aft	aft	aft	aft	mrn	mrn	mrn	aft	aft
	Waterloo 180.........dep.	..	5 27	6 57	8 45	10 45	S X	S O	..	..	12 45	1 15	2 45	..	4 45	5 15	5n45	..	9 45	1 27	5 27
—	Petersfield...........dep.	6 33	7 37	8 50	10 20	12 19	..	..	2 35	2 40	4 18	..	6 35	6 41	7 41	6 17	8 15	1125	3 20	7 20
4½	Rogate, for Harting......	6 43	7 47	9 0	10 30	12 29	..	..	2 45	2 50	4 28	..	6 45	6 51	7 51	6 27	8 25	1135	3 30	7 30
6½	Elsted...............	6 47	7 51	9 7	10 34	12 33	..	..	2 49	2 54	4 32	..	6 49	6 55	7 55	6 31	8 59	1139	3 34	7 34
9½	Midhurst.....{arr.	6 57	8 1	9 20	10 44	12 43	..	..	2 59	4	4 42	..	6 59	5	8 5	6 41	8 59	1149	3 44	7 44
	Midhurst.....{dep.	7 28	8 52	9 43	11 45	1 11	2 45	2 45		4 44	6 45			8 45	..	8 45	1150	3 45	7 45
13	Selham..............	7 36	8 59	9 50	11 52	1 13	2 52	2 52		4 52	6 52			8 52	..	8 52	1157	3 52	7 52
15½	Petworth............	7 43	9 6	9 57	11 59	1 22	2 59	2 59		4 59	6 59			8 59	..	8 58	12 3	3 59	7 59
17½	Fittleworth.........	7 51	9 13	10 6	12 6	1 32	3 6	3 6		5 6	7 6			9 6	..	9 6	12 9	4 6	8 6
20½	Pulborough A.....arr.	7 58	9 21	10 14	12 14	1 40	3 14	3 14		5 14	7 14			9 14	..	9 14	1217	4 14	8 14
70½	London Bridge 249....arr.	9 38	10 40	..	2A11	..	5	3 5A11		7A10	9A11			11A11	..	11A11	..	6A13	10 7
70½	Victoria 249.......... "	9 33	10 31	1153	2 7	40	..	5 7		7 8	9 7			11 7	..	11 7	2 7	5 44	10 20

LONDON, PULBOROUGH, MIDHURST, PETERSFIELD, and LONDON
Third class only between Pulborough and Petersfield

	Up					Week Days												Sundays			
Miles		mrn	mrn	mrn	mrn	mrn	S X	S O	S X	S O	S X	aft	mrn	mrn	mrn	aft	aft
	Victoria 238.........dep.	..	..	5*20	6A18	9 18	9 18	48	11 48	12 18	1 48	2 18	3 48	4 8	6N18	7 46	10 48	3 48	7 18
	London Bridge 238.... "	..	5 25	A	2A9	A15	10A36	11A31	12A*15	..	2A18	3A31	4A17	5A48	7 40	10 16	..	6A155
	Pulborough ....dep.	..	7 56	8 15	10 25	12 35	1 56	..	3 35	3 35	5 35	5 35	7 35	..	9 35	12 33	3 30	8 35
2½	Fittleworth........	..	8 2	8 22	10 41	12 41	2 2		3 42	3 42	5 41	5 41	7 41		9 41	12 40	5 36	8 41
5½	Petworth...........	..	8 8	8 28	10 47	12 47	2 9		3 47	3 47	5 47	5 47	7 47		9 47	12 46	3 42	8 47
7½	Selham....{arr.	..	8 14	8 36	10 53	12 53	2 15		3 53	3 53	5 53	5 53	7 53		9 53	12 52	5 48	8 53
11	Midhurst.....{arr.	..	8 22	8 44	11 0	1 0	2 24		4 1	4 1	6 0	6 0	8 0		10 0	12 59	5 57	9 0
	Midhurst.....{dep.	7 8	8 11	..	9 33	11 2	1 2	3 46	3 46	5 2	5 2	7 10	7 10	8 11	7 28	10 2	1 0	6 42	9 1
14½	Elsted.............	7 17	8 20	..	9 42	11 11	1 11	3 55	3 55	5 11	5 11	7 19	7 19	8 20	7 37	1011	1 9	6 51	9 10
16½	Rogate, for Harting......	7 21	8 24	..	9 46	11 15	1 15	3 59	3 59	5 15	5 15	7 23	7 23	8 24	7 41	1015	1 13	6 55	9 14
10½	Petersfield.......arr.	7 32	8 35	..	9 57	11 26	1 26	4 10	5 26	5 26	7 34	7 34	8 35	7 52	1026	1 24	7 6	9 25
70½	Waterloo 181........arr.	9 13	10 0	..	12 31	1 1	3 1	6 19	6 19	7 1	7 1	10 19	10 19	1119	1016	12 1	3 16	9 1	11 19

NOTES

A Third class only.
* Change at East Croydon.
† Change at Sutton.

A Station for Storrington (5 miles).
B Arr. 11 46 mrn on Sats.
N Dep. 5 48 aft on Sats
n Dep. 5 27 aft on Sats.
S O Saturday only
S X Saturdays excepted
X Change at East Croydon. Dep. 5B31 aft on Sats.

1942

117. Exhibiting a 75D (Horsham) shed plate, class E4 no. 32469 pauses between shunting operations to replenish its tanks, on 21st December 1960. Freight services came to an end in October 1964, after a brief period of operation by class 33 diesel locomotives. (D. Fereday Glenn)

119. W.L. West & Sons expanded their business into the goods shed, office and entire yard. The shed replaced a smaller structure in 1902 and was demolished in August 1986, to make way for a Wimpey housing estate. It contained a 1½-ton capacity crane and in the yard there was one with a 10-ton lift. (D. Dornom)

120. This sad view is included to show the railings round the subway steps and the relationship between the station and the present houses, nos. 2 and 4 Bourne Way. Flats and houses now occupy the site. (C. White)

118. A ramblers' excursion on 8th June 1958 and this LCGB railtour on 24th June 1962 are believed to have been the only passenger carrying trains since regular services ceased (apart from the final one on 18th October 1964, seen in picture no. 36). Class E6 no. 32417 and E4 no. 32503 made a memorable sight as they emerged from the east of the tunnel into the beautiful West Sussex countryside. (D. Fereday Glenn)

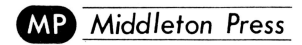

MP *Middleton Press*

Easebourne Lane, Midhurst, West Sussex, GU29 9AZ
☎ Midhurst (073 081) 3169

BRANCH LINES

SOUTH COAST RAILWAYS

SOUTHERN MAIN LINES

STEAMING THROUGH

OTHER RAILWAY BOOKS

OTHER BOOKS